Words Worth Writing

100 Positive Words for Recapturing the Art of Cursive Handwriting

By
Tara D. Turner

This Book Belongs to:

_____

Dedicated to:

Both of my #browneyedgirls

Alecsys Jianni Proctor Turner (daughter)

&

Mary Jacquelyn Cambridge Porter (mother)

ISBN 9781733800020

Why Words Worth Writing?

If you've ever seen the movie Monster's Inc. you may remember that the main characters had a nightly scare goal to reach. They had to capture a certain number of children's screams because scream energy powered their existence. (spoiler alert) The end of the movie actually revealed that the laughter of children had more power than their screams. From then on, they only sought out genuine laughter as an energy source.

What does that have to do with cursive writing? Well, as a Montessori teacher, I often remind my students that energy is all around us, both good and bad. There is a certain energy associated with word power and positive words just like laughter, are more powerful than negative words.

The *Words Worth Writing Series* is a way for intermediate writes to practice cursive writing while being exposed to positive adjectives and adverbs. Some of the word energy will come as reminders and some will be introductions. Either way using these words can only brighten and elevate writing choices. Speaking and writing will be improved as a result of experiencing *Words Worth Writing*.

Good penmanship and handwriting skills are essential for nonverbal expression. Cursive, script or longhand, are all words that describe a dying art form in communication. Signing an autograph, opening a business and cashing a million-dollar check all require the use of a cursive signature.

How to Use This Workbook?

On the pages to come, the cursive alphabet will get you going. Carefully trace each letter. Each page thereafter will contain a positive word, it's definition, and space for a little practice. Each page contains a quote from a famous/important person using the word in context. Before turning each page, try using the word in your own cursive sentence. Enjoy!

Carefully trace each letter

Aa Bb Cc Dd Ee

Ff Gg Hh Ii Jj

Kk Ll Mm Nn

Oo Pp Qq Rr Ss

Tt Uu Vv Ww

Xx Yy Zz

Carefully trace each letter

Aa Bb Cc Dd Ee

Ff Gg Hh Ii Jj

Kk Ll Mm Nn

Oo Pp Qq Rr Ss

Tt Uu Vv Ww

Xx Yy Zz

------unapologetic------

Definition: having absolutely no regret. Bold.

unapologetic

unapologetic

unapologetic

unapologetic

Being unapologetic means that I will be all of me. I will no longer shrink or compromise myself by playing small so others will not feel insecure in my presence.

-Lisa Nichols

-----peaceful-----

Definition: a trait that characterizes a person as tranquil or free from malice or strife

peaceful

peaceful

peaceful

peaceful

Those who make
peaceful
revolution
impossible will
make violent
revolution
inevitable.

-John F. Kennedy

------forgiving------

Definition: a characteristic that allows a person to forgive those who have wronged them.

forgiving

forgiving

forgiving

forgiving

A forgiving heart will beat long after the whispers of breath are no more.

-Dr. W.F. Payne

------motivational------

Definition: able to inspire or encourage thoughts or actions from others

motivational

motivational

motivational

motivational

The loudest motivational voice in your life may come from a silent supporter.

-Mary L. Cambridge

-----beautiful-----

Definition: having traits that are pleasing to the senses

beautiful

beautiful

beautiful

beautiful

Keep smiling,
because life is a
beautiful thing
and there's so
much to smile
about.

-Marilyn Monroe

-----encouraging-----

Definition: having the ability to motivate others with words or actions

encouraging

encouraging

encouraging

encouraging

For me, life is about being positive and hopeful, choosing to be joyful, choosing to be encouraging, choosing to be empowering.

-Billy Porter

------authentic-----

Definition: genuine or unchanged by outside factors

authentic

authentic

authentic

authentic

> There's power in allowing yourself to be known and heard, in owning your unique story, in using your authentic voice. And there's grace in being willing to know and hear others.
>
> **-Michelle Obama**

------flawless------

Definition: having no blemishes or imperfections

flawless

flawless

flawless

flawless

To speak in literature with the perfect rectitude and insouciance of the movements of animals and the unimpeachable of the sentiment of trees in the woods and grass by the roadside is the flawless triumph of art.

-Walt Whitman

-----magnificent-----

Definition: existing in excellence, impressively beautiful or extraordinary

magnificent

magnificent

magnificent

magnificent

The ocean is so magnificent, peaceful and awesome - the rest of the world disappears for me when I'm on a wave.
-Paul Walker

-----successful-----

Definition: able to achieve greatness; accomplished

successful

successful

successful

successful

If you want to be successful, you have to jump, there's no way around it. When you jump, I can assure you that your parachute will not open right away. But if you do not jump, your parachute will never open. If you're safe, you'll never soar!

-Steve Harvey

------marvelous------

Definition: being extraordinary; displaying splendid characteristics

marvelous

marvelous

marvelous

marvelous

Even with all of the things that are so awful, if you walk into your yard and stay there looking at almost anything for five minutes, you will be stunned by how marvelous life is and how incredibly lucky we are to have it.

-Alice Walker

-----talented-----

Definition: possessing natural gifts or exceptional skill in a particular area

talented

talented

talented

talented

Genius is one percent inspiration and ninety-nine percent perspiration. As a result, a genius is often a talented person who has simply done all of his homework.

-Thomas A. Edison

-----savvy-----

Definition: possessing an elevated skill level naturally

savvy

savvy

savvy

savvy

> A savvy entrepreneur will not always look for investment money, first.
>
> **-Daymond John**

-----articulate-----

Definition: having the ability to speak fluently with clarity

articulate

articulate

articulate

articulate

Silence the artist
and you have
silenced the most
articulate voice
the people have.

−Katharine Hepburn.

-----professional-----

Definition: of a high standard in behavior, appearance, speech and skill

professional

professional

professional

professional

Professional is not a label you give yourself. It's a description you hope others will apply to you."

-David Maister

------loyal------

Definition: leaving no question to allegiance

loyal

loyal

loyal

loyal

One loyal friend
is worth ten
thousand
relatives

-Euripides

-----confident-----

Definition: showing a high level of certainty or being self assured

confident

confident

confident

confident

There is nothing more beautiful than a confident woman.

-Suze Orman

-----ambitious-----

Definition: having a strong desire for success and achievement

ambitious

ambitious

ambitious

ambitious

Don't be afraid to be ambitious about your goals. Hard work never stops. Neither should your dreams.

-Dwayne Johnson

(The Rock)

-----compassionate----

Definition: feeling or showing genuine concern for others

compassionate

compassionate

compassionate

compassionate

When the people become involved in their government, government becomes more accountable, and our society is stronger, more compassionate, and better prepared for the challenges of the future.

-Arnold Schwarzenegger

-----generous-----

Definition: freely giving of time, money or other kind offerings to others

generous

generous

generous

generous

Above all things, lose no occasion of exercising your dispositions to be grateful, to be generous, to be charitable, to be humane, to be true, just, firm, orderly, courageous, etc. Consider every act of this kind as an exercise which will strengthen your moral faculties and increase your worth.

-Thomas Jefferson

-----innovative-----

Definition: having original ideas and drive to create newness

innovative

innovative

innovative

innovative

A person with an innovative spirit can create, motivate and invent new ideas.

-M. Jacquelyn Porter

-----amazing-----

Definition: having wonderful and impressive qualities

amazing

amazing

amazing

amazing

If you are always
trying to be
normal, you will
never know how
amazing
you can be.
-Maya Angelou

------sincere-----

Definition: genuine; honest; free from deceit

sincere

sincere

sincere

sincere

It doesn't matter what you believe just as long as you're sincere.

-Charles M. Schulz

-----resourceful-----

Definition: having the ability to overcome things that hinder to progress

resourceful

resourceful

resourceful

resourceful

Life's too short to hang out with people who aren't resourceful.

-Jeff Bezos

-----courageous-----

Definition: showing bravery

courageous

courageous

courageous

courageous

You must be bold, brave, and courageous and find a way...to get in the way.

-John Lewis

-----discreet-----

Definition: showing caution and care with behavior or sensitive information

discreet

discreet

discreet

discreet

I am a very
discreet human
when it comes to
other people.

-Carrie Fisher

------hospitable------

Definition: description of someone who takes pride in making others feel welcome

hospitable

hospitable

hospitable

hospitable

The human soul is hospitable and will entertain conflicting sentiments and contradictory opinions with much impartiality.

- Mary Ann Evans
George Eliot
(pen name)

-----worthy-----

Definition: deserving of honor

worthy

worthy

worthy

worthy

If you want to win, don't compete, because once you decide they are worthy of competing with, they have already won.

-Kobe Bryant

------masterful-----

Definition: skillful and powerful

masterful

masterful

masterful

masterful

Godzilla was the most masterful of all dinosaur movies because it made you believe it was really happening.

-Steven Spielberg

------diligent-----

Definition: showing extreme focus on work

diligent

diligent

diligent

diligent

The diligent farmer plants trees, of which he, himself, will never see the fruit.

-Roman Proverb

------independent-----

Definition: needing no authority figure to obtain achievement

independent

independent

independent

independent

My mother told me to be a lady. For her, that meant to be your own person, be independent.

-Ruth Bader Ginsburg

------fair------

Definition: a person that follows all rules and upholds ideas of equality

fair

fair

fair

fair

The truth is that the vast majority of Americans are good, fair, and just, and they want their country to reflect those ideals.

-Kamala Harris

------intellectual-----

Definition: possessing superior thinking

intellectual

intellectual

intellectual

intellectual

The fact that man knows right from wrong proves his intellectual superiority to the other creatures; but the fact that he can do wrong proves his moral inferiority to any creatures that cannot.

-Mark Twain

-----scholarly-----

Definition: one who possess a serious attitude about academics

scholarly

scholarly

scholarly

scholarly

But the dust! And the clutter! My housewifely and scholarly instincts were equally offended.

-Barbara Mertz

------optimistic-----

Definition: a characteristic that describes people who see the bright side of things

optimistic

optimistic

optimistic

optimistic

When I get impatient, I get very optimistic about the things I see ahead.

-Bill Gates

-----dynamic-----

Definition: having a positive attitude and is full of energy and ideas

dynamic

dynamic

dynamic

dynamic

I think that my strong determination for justice comes from the very strong, dynamic personality of my father.

-Dr. Martin Luther King, Jr.

------thoughtful-----

Definition: being considerate of the feelings of others; thinking of the well being of others

thoughtful

thoughtful

thoughtful

thoughtful

My guiding principles in life are to be honest, genuine, thoughtful and caring.

-Prince William

-----cautious-----

Definition: careful to consider all options

cautious

cautious

cautious

cautious

The cautious
seldom err.

- Confucius

----understanding----

Definition: having the ability to sympathize and forgive

understanding

understanding

understanding

understanding

Love is not all that is required in a relationship. It needs understanding, openness, kindness, patience, long-suffering

- Iyanla Vanzant

-----dedicated-----

Definition: showing devotion to a person, task, or purpose

dedicated

dedicated

dedicated

dedicated

I need to be surrounded by people as passionate and as dedicated as I am.

-Lauryn Hill

------unique------

Definition: one of a kind; having no comparable other

unique

unique

unique

unique

Always remember that you are absolutely unique just like everyone else.
-Margaret Mead

-----powerful-----

Definition: exhibiting great control over people's thoughts or actions

Powerful the man that gets more done dead than alive.

-Katori Hall

------admirable-----

Definition: having qualities that are respected

admirable

admirable

admirable

admirable

By far the greatest and most admirable form of wisdom is that needed to plan and beautify cities and human communities.

-Socrates

-----eloquent-----

Definition: impressive and expressive through speaking

eloquent

eloquent

eloquent

eloquent

Eloquent speech
is not from
lip to ear, but
rather from heart
to heart.

-William Jennings Bryan

-----philanthropic-----

Definition: seeking to promote quality living through generous donations

philanthropic

philanthropic

philanthropic

philanthropic

I have tried to hold my philanthropic passion to fashion, because I think this is very important, and I realize I need to delve even deeper into it.

-Donna Karan

------affluent-----

Definition: having significant resources, money, or wealth

affluent

affluent

affluent

affluent

In the affluent society, no useful distinction can be made between luxuries and necessities.

-John Kenneth Galbraith

------imaginative------

Definition: showing ingenuity and creativity with no limitations

imaginative

imaginative

imaginative

imaginative

It will be found, in fact, that the ingenious are always fanciful, and the truly imaginative never otherwise than analytic.

-Edgar Allan Poe

-----respectful-----

Definition: showing deference; having admiration for someone or something

respectful

respectful

respectful

respectful

We don't need to share the same opinions as others, but we need to be respectful.

-Taylor Swift

-----impressive-----

Definition: having characteristics of evoking awe or admiration

impressive

impressive

impressive

impressive

I love New York, it's always been my home. It has everything - music, fashion, entertainment, impressive buildings, huge parks, street cafes.

-Puff Daddy

-----inspiring-----

Definition: having the ability to urge someone to think or act

inspiring

inspiring

inspiring

inspiring

Being able to
motivate yourself
is the only way to
be truly inspiring
to others.

-Ben Guilford

------charming------

Definition: describes one who masters the art of being pleasant and delightful

charming

charming

charming

charming

A woman can be sexy, charming, witty, or shy with her shoes.

-Christian Louboutin

-----strong-----

Definition: possessing qualities that suggest the likelihood of success

strong

strong

strong

strong

The weak fall, but the strong will remain and never go under!

-Anne Frank

------adorable------

Definition: one able to inspire great affection; possessing a cuteness

adorable

adorable

adorable

adorable

When grace is joined with wrinkles, it is adorable. There is an unspeakable dawn in happy old age.

-Victor Hugo

-----jovial-----

Definition: having a joy that cannot be extinguished

jovial

jovial

jovial

jovial

Our jovial star reigned at his birth.

-William Shakespeare

-----artistic-----

Definition: having a natural affinity to visual, performing, and other types of art

artistic

artistic

artistic

artistic

Since I was young, the artistic expression that fashion embodies has inspired me. It's a way to communicate one's self.

-Maria Sharapova

-----enchanting-----

Definition: able to captivate as if by magical spell

enchanting

enchanting

enchanting

enchanting

Now I really feel the landscape, I can be bold and include every tone of pink and blue: it's enchanting, it's delicious, and I hope it will please you.

-Claude Monet

------vibrant-----

Definition: bright and colorful; full of energy

vibrant

vibrant

vibrant

vibrant

Your attitude is like the mind's paintbrush. It can paint everything in bright, vibrant colors-creating a masterpiece.

-John C. Maxwell

-----invincible-----

Definition: unable to be defeated

invincible

invincible

invincible

invincible

When virtuous and knowledgeable women grace the endeavor with their sweet love, then it is invincible.

-Jose Marti

-----awesome-----

Definition: extremely impressive

awesome

awesome

awesome

awesome

People always tell you, 'Be humble. Be humble.' When was the last time someone told you to be amazing? Be great! Be great! Be awesome!

-Kanye West

------unstoppable------

Definition: qualities that inspire dedication and an unwillingness to quit

unstoppable

unstoppable

unstoppable

unstoppable

Life takes on meaning when you become motivated, set goals and charge after them in an unstoppable manner.

-Les Brown

------devoted-----

Definition: describes a person that is loyal, committed or dedicated

devoted

devoted

devoted

devoted

Every bit of me is devoted to love and art. And I aspire to try to be a teacher to my young fans who feel just like I felt when I was younger. I want to free them (My young fans) of their fears and make them feel that they can make their own space in the world.

-Lady Gaga

-------ingenious-------

Definition: one who possesses exceptional intellect

ingenious

ingenious

ingenious

ingenious

Oprah Winfrey represents the most ingenious and creative expression of black spiritual genius in the public mainstream that we've had in quite a long time, if ever.

-Michael Eric Dyson

------magical------

Definition: exciting and beautiful; unexplainable by natural definitions

magical

magical

magical

magical

Magical places are always beautiful and deserve to be contemplated ... Always stay on the bridge between the invisible and the visible.

-Paulo Coelho

-----decadent-----

Definition: luxuriously self indulgent

decadent

decadent

decadent

decadent

When I got my success, I became decadent for a while. This was 2003 to 2008. I fell for tiramisu really hard.

-Jill Scott

-----impeccable-----

Definition: a description of a character without fault

impeccable

impeccable

impeccable

impeccable

My father is a man of impeccable character who has worked tirelessly for the United Nations for many years. His integrity is beyond reproach.

-Kojo Annan

-----enthusiastic-----

Definition: showing unmatched energy and eager enjoyment

enthusiastic

enthusiastic

enthusiastic

enthusiastic

We're just enthusiastic about what we do!

-Steve Jobs

-----mesmerizing-----

Definition: able to magically capture the attention of an audience of one or many

mesmerizing

mesmerizing

mesmerizing

mesmerizing

The language of a smile is charming, mesmerizing, meaningful, and often mysterious, but everyone understands a smile better than words.

–Debasish Mridha

------lavish------

Definition: luxurious, extravagant, and generous

lavish

lavish

lavish

lavish

I'm a little lavish I must admit. But I'm not really concerned with money.

Being rich is not my goal, being wealthy is.

-Cee Lo Green

------exciting-----

Definition: having an enthusiastic, energetic personality

exciting

exciting

exciting

exciting

If your goal isn't scary and exciting, then it's not a big enough goal for you.

- Bob Proctor

-----remarkable-----

Definition: being worthy of attention

remarkable

remarkable

remarkable

remarkable

You're either remarkable or invisible. Make a choice.

-Seth Godin

-----gifted-----

Definition: possessing a natural gift or ability

gifted

gifted

gifted

gifted

The gifted man bears his gifts into the world, not for his own benefit, but for the people among whom he is placed; for the gifts are not his, he himself is a gift to the community.

-Henry Ford

-----phenomenal-----

Definition: extraordinary in character; greatness unexplainable by science

phenomenal

phenomenal

phenomenal

phenomenal

Be phenomenal
or be forgotten!

-Eric Thomas

-----prepared-----

Definition: one who takes advance steps to be ready

prepared

prepared

prepared

prepared

It's better to be prepared than to get ready.

-Will Smith

-----athletic-----

Definition: one who excels in physical aptitude

athletic

athletic

athletic

athletic

Friendships born on the field of athletic strife are the real gold of competition. Awards become corroded; friends gather no dust.

-Jesse Owens

-----ethical-----

Definition: describes people who engage in activities or make decisions based on moral principles

ethical

ethical

ethical

ethical

Without "ethical culture", there is no salvation for humanity.

-Albert Einstein

-----reflective-----

Definition: a quality related to deep thinking; one who is considerate or compassionate

reflective

reflective

reflective

reflective

The more reflective you are, the more effective you are.

-Pete and Alisa

----extraordinary----

Definition: above and beyond that which is considered normal

extraordinary

extraordinary

extraordinary

extraordinary

The difference between ordinary and extraordinary is that little extra.

-Jimmy Johnson

------brilliant-----

Definition: exceptional in intellect or talent

brilliant

brilliant

brilliant

brilliant

> We ask ourselves, who am I to be brilliant, gorgeous, talented, fabulous? Actually, who are you not to be?"
>
> **-Marianne Williamson**

-----creative-----

Definition: having original thoughts and ideas

creative

creative

creative

creative

Every man must
decide whether
he will walk in
the light of
creative altruism
or the darkness
of destructive
selfishness.

-Dr. Martin Luther King, Jr.

-----assertive-----

Definition: showing confidence and strength

assertive

assertive

assertive

assertive

Be assertive not aggressive and your road will be far less bumpy.

-Shel Givens

------melodious------

Definition: being associated with the beautiful melody in music

melodious

melodious

melodious

melodious

Your voice is a reflection of your melodious soul.

-Shristy Sinha

-----trustworthy-----

Definition: having qualities that can be trusted

trustworthy

trustworthy

trustworthy

trustworthy

You become a Leader when people trust you. Being trustworthy is the biggest quality of a Leader.

-Anonymous

------pleasant------

Definition: having a charming personality and demeanor

pleasant

pleasant

pleasant

pleasant

A pleasant smile can cure an ill situation and mend a broken friendship.

-John Day

-----organized-----

Definition: describes those who maximize the use of time and space through order

organized

organized

organized

organized

Being organized
is a sign of self-
respect.

-Gabrielle Bernstein

-----fascinating-----

Definition: proving to be of extreme interest

fascinating

fascinating

fascinating

fascinating

Being good in business is the most fascinating kind of art.

- Andy Warhol

------logical-----

Definition: capable of sound reasoning

logical

logical

logical

logical

Chess can help a child develop logical thinking, decision making, reasoning, and pattern recognition skills, which in turn can help math and verbal skills.

-Susan Polgar

-----affectionate-----

Definition: able to display affection without unreadiness

affectionate

affectionate

affectionate

affectionate

Be a good human being, a warmhearted, affectionate person.

That is my fundamental belief.

-Dalai Lama

------favorable------

Definition: showing traits that are appealing and generally approved

favorable

favorable

favorable

favorable

If one does not know to which port one is sailing, no wind is favorable.

-Lucius Annaeus Seneca

----unforgettable----

Definition: one who leaves positive marks on the memory; impossible to forget

unforgettable

unforgettable

unforgettable

unforgettable

Hospitality and cooking are my passion, and

I love nothing more than seeing someone's face when they taste an unforgettable bite.

-Ayesha Curry

-----musical-----

Definition: skilled in the delivery or understanding of music

musical

musical

musical

musical

Any child who is properly trained can develop musical ability just as all children develop the ability to speak their mother tongue.

-Shinichi Suzuki

------humorous------

Definition: characterized by causing laughter or displaying a sense of humor

humorous

humorous

humorous

humorous

A humorous person has the natural ability to make you laugh.

-Unknown

-----eclectic-----

Definition: having style, ideas, or collections based on a broad range of sources

eclectic

eclectic

eclectic

eclectic

I like the idea of an eclectic approach, incorporating jazz with other forms and other genres of music.

-Herbie Hancock

--------compatible--------

Definition: able to coexist without conflict

compatible

compatible

compatible

compatible

We are all a little weird and life's a little weird, and when we find someone whose weirdness is compatible with ours, we join up with them and fall in mutual weirdness and call it love.

-Dr. Seuss

-----perfect-----

Definition: having all traits necessary for the best outcome

perfect

perfect

perfect

perfect

If everything

was perfect, you would never learn and you would never grow.

-Beyonce Knowles

------fabulous-----

Definition: extraordinarily wonderful

fabulous

fabulous

fabulous

fabulous

A girl should be two things: classy and fabulous.

-Coco Chanel

-----effervescent-----

Definition: having a bubbly personality

effervescent

effervescent

effervescent

effervescent

She may be the most energetic woman I've ever met. I just marvel at her optimism and her ability to get things done. She just can't be contained. She's bubbly beyond effervescent.

-Vin Scully

-----determined-----

Definition: one who has laser focus on a desired outcome

determined

determined

determined

determined

A determined
mind and a
strong will bear
endless
possibilities.

-Unknown

-----persistent-----

Definition: a character trait associated with those who stay the course

persistent

persistent

persistent

persistent

It's only those who are persistent, and willing to study things deeply, who achieve the Master Work.

-Paulo Coehlo

------charismatic------

Definition: exercising a magic-like charm that evokes loyalty in action and or thought

charismatic

charismatic

charismatic

charismatic

Being charismatic doesn't make you a leader. Being a leader makes you charismatic.

-Seth Godin

-----courteous-----

Definition: describes a person that performs at the highest level of respect, honor and courtesy

courteous

courteous

courteous

courteous

> When you smile, you don't only appear to be more likable and courteous, you appear to be more competent.
>
> **-Ron Gutman**

www.ingramcontent.com/pod-product-compliance
Lightning Source LLC
Chambersburg PA
CBHW081257040426
42452CB00014B/2537